hues in ink

Vaanee Tripathi

Leadstart
INKSTATE

ISBN: 978-93-5610-611-6

First published in India 2022 by Leadstart Inkstate
A brand of One Point Six Technologies Pvt. Ltd.

123, Building J2, Shram Seva Premises,
Wadala Truck Terminal,
Mumbai 400022, Maharashtra, INDIA
Phone: +91 96999 33000
Email: info@leadstartcorp.com
www.leadstartcorp.com

Editor: Shayoni Mitra
Cover: Ilaya Raja
Layouts: Kevis Tech

to Ruhi and Veer,
my rays of sunlight on a dark
winter evening. I love you.
Always and forever.

"Words mean more than what is set down in paper, it takes the human voice to infuse them with a deeper meaning."

- Maya Angelou

CONTENTS

AUTHOR'S BIO

Vaanee Tripathi is a 17-year-old student who comes from the eastern suburbs of Delhi, India. She lives in a family of 5 with her parents and two younger siblings. Her passion for poetry started at the age of 9 and while not very good at it then, she stuck with it. She conceptualized this book at the age of 14 and has been building it brick by brick, verse by verse ever since. Apart from poetry, she enjoys reading fiction and can often be found nestled in the pages of a book.

Vaanee is also a trained kathak dancer and enjoys the art form thoroughly. Academically, she is inclined towards the sciences and is currently studying the same.

With this book, she forays into the published media, a journey she truly looks forward to.

ACKNOWLEDGEMENT

Thank you.

Yes, you, the person reading this.

If you're reading this, it means you've taken time out of your lives and spent it with my poems… and time, isn't it the most precious thing to give? Hence, I thank you truly and with all I have. You're now a part of my journey, one which I hope makes both of us understand this world a little better. I hope while reading this book you find a verse that will stick with you or one which will make you think… or maybe one that will just make you smile.

I don't know how the world functions. Is there a god? Gods? Or is it just the culmination of the permutations and combinations of some set scientific equations? Is it both? Or is it just a dream? I don't think anybody knows… but I do firmly believe that there is some great power above me that is too advanced for us to even comprehend, and here, I thank that divine force for giving me the gift of words and the intention to construct this little piece of my life. I am truly grateful.

Writing is hard, publishing is harder. Keeping aside the logistical and creative work that goes in, it also takes immense courage. Courage to let yourself be vulnerable in front of the world. Courage I didn't think I had in me… courage that my loved ones built. I don't think I say this enough to them, but, thank you.

Thank you, maa for your unconditional belief in me. You have more faith in me than I have in myself and that is what drives me to do my best. Thank you for telling me that failure is okay, that flaws are okay, imperfections are okay and that it's the effort that matters. Thank you for setting me right when I was lagging, for the occasional reprimanding – I kind of needed that too and for not letting me give up without trying. And most of all, for the love and trust.

Thank you, dad for the affection, care and the unwavering support; for showing me since my childhood, that it's okay to do something different, to pursue my passion, to take 'the road not taken' that is. Thank you for checking in to see if I was okay, every time I wrote a sad poem. I know I didn't say it, but it warms my heart to see you so genuinely concerned. It always made me smile. Thank you, both of you, for applauding and encouraging the 9-year-old child for her poems, even though they were nowhere near decent it was what made me do better. I love you.

A huge shout-out to all my friends who have read these poems, cheered me on, and were nothing but absolute sweethearts. You know who you guys are. I love you too, from the core of my heart.

Last but not least, the entire team at Leadstart. It wouldn't have been possible without you guys. Thank you for all your efforts towards making some 25 odd poems into a collection, a book. I know I am not the easiest person to work with but thank you for bearing with me, for being patient enough to dwell over every period, comma, line, and word with me, for letting me change things a million times and for being with me every step of the way. This book is what it is today because of the many people who added parts of themselves in it and I cannot even begin to explain how grateful I am to you for the same. Thank you for bringing my dream to the bookshelves, it was a pleasure working with each and every one of you.

And with this I give you, “Hues in Ink”, a piece of my heart which has consumed every inch of my being for almost three years now. The moment you picked this book up it became just as much yours as it is mine, be gentle with it.

1

La Noire – The Shade of Tartarus

Tartarus – The infinite abyss. The ancient Greeks envisaged a place beneath the underworld, a place as far away from the land of Hades as heaven is from the earth. The land of the infernal, the satanic, and the vicious; the manifestation of sheer darkness. A place where one's coffin is just the first stair to an eternity of pain and torment... A place that daunts Death himself, quivering with depravity and a hypnotic draw. Like all myths and mythological tales, I like to believe this has a greater and a more profound meaning than just this. Perhaps the ancient Greeks were referring to the darkness which nests within all of us... the emotions which lure us towards them with such vigour that defiance is futile. The place within ourselves where our demons dwell. The thoughts which propel us down a spiral to confines we don't know how to escape. Black or *la noire* (in French) is a shade that tells a very similar tale to me. A tale of obscurity, despair, desolation succumbing to which agonizes one more than death ever could.

Bleeding Behind the Fastened Gates

In those misty eyes,
In those deceiving loves,
In those bygone highs
In those withered hopes

In those, whose each smile buries their tears
In those hidden behind their fastened gates
In those who wander the edge reigned by fear
In those, for whom the twilight just never wanes…

In those hearts who wrestle the past of fate
In those hearts with memories the shade of grey
In those hearts hushed through the drift of dates
In those heart on peeking in which, the midnight shies away

It is their truth they veil from their self;
It is what lives off the bygone them, from the bygone days
It is what exhausts the each sunset to mull
It is what engulfs every inch of them, a thousand times and more.

Pain scorches their soul, trauma charred their minds,
A searing labyrinth engulfs their beings
Only to unravel more with every second piercing by.
The insidious evil pulling the ropes… scarring their heart…
Never letting go.

They sit astound, letting the torrents of time drown them.
They never heal, only so sparsely numb; like a blade
that has forgotten the finesse of murder.
Waiting to arouse the memories which sleep sound
of the light they lost, and how far they've gone
by those blazing stars above

A Year in Hell

Summer / the scorching heat
Roused by his blistering caress,
My spirit parched for tears to cascade
wolved my esteem down my breath
like a vagrant, in the wilderness, astray.
Choking on water's fleeting trace

I shroud myself in webs of words
To escape from feeling bare
His piercing eyes strip me down
Until I am nothing but his –
suffocating to his lust and animus

Monsoon / the torrential floods
I lose myself like a drop in his ocean
I drown and thrash and flail
Sinking further and more and more
Till my world above grows obscure
Like a half-forgotten memory…

Grapple with the current, to stand upright
These showers from the sky escape their ties
only to be shackled once more by the earth.
And hence, what use is it to escape?

Autumn/ the shedding leaves
Engulfed in fiery hues, I lose my flame
Flustered by this breeze, I lose my thoughts
Reigned by him, I lose my self;
When his hands clasp mine and I cannot let go
Bit by bit, each night, every night.

I wake up to these roads heaped in leaves
And my mind immersed in shame
A nervous robin chirruping on the sill
But my mind deafened by its own roar

Winter/ the freezing blizzard
The earth bleeds white in its freezing milieu
losing the life which coursed through its veins
And yet I lose more – sensations
of pain and of grief...
Time stands still in this misty winter land
but then why does the day wither into the night?
only to end my respite

the freezing breeze weighed down, with pity flows free
the skeletal trees break free from their slumber;
in wait for a blossom.
Yet here I am caged in a world
That has forgotten to live in spring.

In These Last Moments

1…2…3.
A flicker, slight, sending the flame cowering
To the wick on the funereal cierge.
I hold on to my breath
Strained, scarce and slow
But like the flame, it handles yet another blow.

1…2…3
The air, heavy with lavender
Like one sunset rendezvous
under the lilac sky,
when she slipped through my hands
like the spools of fine silk
to get lost in the fields of
reminiscent memoirs…
The Past now has cornered me in the cell
of my melancholy and solitude

1…2…3
In these last moments,
Death is an old fiend I yearn.
Lost loves and lost times
Haunt my bedside
But where do you run to now?
When you're already at the very end?

1…2…3
The smouldering candle now barely seen
Every bit of wax that melts
Stretches my life too thin…
Like the last fibril of
a fickle yarn.
Flashes of life on a dizzy carousel
Painted with feigned efforts and
Erratic adieus.
Which is why I let go
Alone, in this dark and dusty room.

2 La Grise – The Shade of An Unbridled Perspective

To live in this age, immersed in conflicts – both internal and external, and vices – both evil and necessary, unwavering, intransient belief systems become almost futile. Right and wrong, moral and immoral, are left as hollow constructs with no material application. There is good in evil and evil in good. To pinpoint the truly ethical becomes more challenging with every passing strife. Grey or *La Grise* is a confluence of black and white, a colour that enunciates that there's nothing that's absolute in this world. It is the shade of acceptance – to accept that no person is free from the fetters of flaws; of balance – amongst the darker and the lighter hues in life; of discovery – of your Self and of perspectives, which you realize are fluid, as well as of turmoil, unrest, and disorder – in the material world as well as in one's mind.

Confines from Our Minds

We live in a world where the borders pervade maps.
Like creases on a visage
that has drifted along
the caress of age.
Concocted from nihility.
amidst lands and amidst people,
venom seethes just a step away.

We live in a world where the lines that seclude
Moral from immoral are obscured
just a little more each day.
Where war wages over
right and wrong: transient
like mere wisps of smoke.
An illusive theory and
a reassuring mirage

We live in a world where we are moulded,
By the subtle strokes
of a veiled caucus.
To embrace a precept to
perceive the globe
As black and white,
amongst a race that bleeds grey...

Not a Heartbreaker

The screen lit up with your text.
Just another one among a myriad of those
Should I say?
My mind now a bustling bazaar
Astir with retorts...
Picking ones which I hope will
bruise you the least.

That day when you blurted, "I love you"
I hurdled a barrage of words, just not
the ones you wanted me to.
looked around to see the shattered remnants
of the heart, I crushed, and our friendship too
but that was all done by you

Now I walk these aisles burdened
with all the eyes on me
every rustle, every speck, every whisper
pleads your case for you
coercing love, as if it's nothing but
a snow globe with two tiny beings

You text me daily, I rarely reply.
You save me a seat; I sit on the one behind
You drown in nostalgia; I pretend not to have seen
I come up for some air, you pummel me back in.
You say you love me; I say I never did
Your eyes swim in despair, my heart now engulfed in guilt

Anger surging in my veins but I bury it deep
Further than my own psyche could see.
I feel like a convict put to trial
Not loving you back, now a felony
But beneath these walls I now hide behind,
Lives a little girl
Who never broke your heart.

Tales I Hear of Me

Dwelling on a stage where
The curtain's never drawn,
A million breaths hover close by.
Every step I take, measured;
Every move I make, critiqued;
losing myself like a dandelion
Amongst a swarm of bees.

Striving to recall my name but
I solely know what they tell me…
Their voices crowd my psych
They build and raise and bolster,
Like a shrine of feathers and
leaves and sprigs
they forge a hollow frame
Of bouquets and flattery

I fall apart like
A billion stars cascading,
and tangle myself
in yarns of what I am supposed to be.
Like a rose,
Its petals stolen by time,
Leaving nothing but just a twig
astray in remembrance

3 La Bleue – The Shade of Sorrow

Sorrow, grief, or despair is an emotion that demands to be felt, for you to surrender yourself to its onslaught. It compels you to dive deeper into your heart, to drench yourself in your grief, to acquaint yourself with melancholy, to find comfort in your tears, and to let yourself be flooded with them, to be overwhelmed with them... Blue or *la bleue,* the shade of icy rains, of weeping skies, of lonely waters, and, of souls in despair. It resonates with sorrow, an emotion purer and deeper than most. While it does depict the feelings of sadness, it also represents serenity, calmness, and peace which you attain once you have traversed the bridges of the feelings you'd kept treasured inside. For me, it stands for the storm and the calm after; the tears and the sleep after; my sad thoughts and my conversations with it after…

On the Brink of Life

That day, the sun, vivid, fiercely glared
Mocking my somber state;
Sat down on the edge, where no one dared…
Except her with her sunken heart
And her erratic fate.

Gazing down below; deafened by the quiet rush,
frantically my mind raced.
Did those lives underneath her feet
entice her to shelter hers?
Or was she too dazed?

I dawdled on the fragile steps
Of the creaking woods,
Hiding the land of Hades;
Only to jump off from the brink of life; safe
Like I wish she did too

I battle with the blazing sun
Who didn't light her soul.
I go to war with the clear sky
Who couldn't efface her storms.
I grapple with Satan himself
Who wouldn't let her free.
And I rip myself to shreds
for I couldn't break her fall…

Her

Those walls, those people
And this barren life,
To the world which passes by,
Every inch still breathes the same.
But these stars above have seen me each night
choking on the tears of change.
The drift of days, the sway of time
and my heart still drowns in blues,
each time when the past hastens by
these streams run all loose
Where sorrow and despair lay intertwined
I felt the thrust of fury at every bit of joy
That dares to lurk around.
Me with my grieving mind…
I had huddled albums, but hushed rooms
stacked cupboards, but vacant days
a plethora of memories, but
a future in absentia;
a new world I cannot turn down and
a dagger stuck right next to my chest
that day which clutches my thoughts too tight…
that day, when she slipped through my hands
like the breeze of time
that day, when she stole her breath
from her very own Self.
That day, when she went all too far away…

Despair Through Droplets

As the hues from the sun receded the canvas above,
The black of sorrow immersed it till I could see
The light of my life, the dazzle of my eyes
abandoned the soul of me
Taking along with him all the reminiscent shades of love

The sky, in a state of absentia; obscure and cloudy,
Without the gleam of the sun and the veil of light.
I too was feeling flawed,
In a daze on which the clouds in me fed;
He had left, pushing me into an abyss of oblivion;
dark and dreary.

The clouds above leaden with a storm waiting to be
unleashed
With tears that hadn't been seen, buried inside somewhere,
I too had a deluge of sorrows, a flurry of emotions,
devouring me up bit by bit.
I yearned to let it surge; I yearned to be eased…

The crackle of thunder rendered the rage of the sky
That mere peal woke up the ground below leaving us all
astound;
My heart too now fazed, plummeting so deep after the high
The newness of it all, the fresh void, and in me the roaring
sounds.

All around me I gaped at the magnificent ruins that rage could inspire
The broken branches, broken roofs and broken dreams all of which someone possessed.
Mine was a broken heart, broken by the fury of fate
Left in smithereens, at its keeper's behest

Looking at these showers, how the sky sought solace in the lands
The mysteries shrouded from the eyes of the world were unveiled
Dwelling to unravel my Self for someone,
to see my secrets stripped and my soul bared,
Walking by the wet winter ways with the rain-washed trees
I submerge myself in a torrent of uproars
Shoved around by masses, dazed in their bygone lives,
Searching to lose my loss amidst the swarm of these reveries...

Each Night, Every Night

The night set in dark
Like a burned down pyre,
The willow rustled
at the caress of the sobs of wind,
You could see her, faintly
As she gazed at the moon,
As if;
waiting for it to come rest in her eyes,
so she could see him among the stars

– Her love

Lonely Skies

The sky, stretching from the beginning of a breath to the end of all else
She shelters the ravaging thunders, pets them
as if coddling an impatient toddler with strokes of tolerance!
She reigns with pride for all those who think of them as mighty,
bask in her and only her glory, and her and only her mercy,
yet one must think or rather wonder
if she lets go of the rains easy…
if she lets the moon be defeated by those blaring rays without hurt
If she then wells up with remorse when the rays too part;
If she witnesses unions and never longs for one;
If she truly is her powerful self
Or just a shell cracking at the earliest question to her being
A soul, without a body
Living in the stories of her grandeur by all who ever lived.

4

La Violette – The Shade of Confluence

Confluences. Unions. A conjunction of disparate entities to create wondrous, new existences. Violette – purple, is a hue born by the confluence of the colours- red and blue. These two elements paint very contrasting images in one's mind. Red is conventionally the shade of fire, passion, lust, anger, love. On the other hand, blue is cold, frigid, and ignorant; the shade of calmness, sorrow, despair, stillness. This chapter talks about emotions like power, which are two-faceted, they kindle a fire and angst in us to excel, but they also bring despair along with them, veiled in the shadows. It is about dreams that drive us to the pinnacle or drive us astray. About differences existing together to create a marvellous vision to behold…

Under the Lilac Skies

We are like the soft drizzle
of the sated skies,
and the parched earth
in wait for the promise
of the tender caress
of the dawn's sparkling tear;
under the morning sun,
so very different
yet a gorgeous sight to behold.

We are like the swift wind
of the autumn rains
scurrying with hushed feet,
and the laden bough of an oak tree
with intertwined arms,
reaching beneath the below.
Under the clear skies,
so very different
yet a melody to listen to

We are like the sun and the moon,
the veiled veracity of this multiverse
and the exposed glaring reality,
the first cry and the last breath
the joy tainted with remorse
and the tears painted in bliss.

We are the dawn and the dusk,
distant
distinct…
but beautiful;
like a kiss
under these lilac skies

Sleep, Little Wolf

Sleep little wolf.
Sleep. Sleep. Sleep.
For the flames, you kindle,
flickering in a violet milieu,
Drunk on mania,
throbbing with voracity
to conquer the ensemble
on the map of three realms and more,
will scare these men too much.

Sleep little wolf.
Sleep. Sleep. Sleep
Keep these eyes shut
for the mad glint in your eyes
and your deafening hoarse roar
with every burning bridge
and every merciless kill
will drive them to insanity.

Sleep little wolf
Sleep. Sleep. Sleep
For these men do not know
how well you will fare
to unscalable heights or to the depths of hell.
And either, gives them nightmare
Sleep, for they cannot.

5 La Rouge – The Shade of Extremes

We feel a multitude of emotions over the course of our lives. If that entire range is taken as a pendulum, then red stands for the two extremes; the sentiments which one feels truly, honestly, earnestly. Love, hate, anger, passion, lust, jealousy are all emotions significantly distinct from each other, yet very similar in one aspect and one aspect only – the vigour with which they are felt, and how they begin commanding every inch of your existence. Red or *la rouge*, talks about the sentiments which dwindle on the very edges of the range of emotions: sheer hatred, the truest love, dripping fury, and the vilest rage. Emotions so strong, that they begin to govern your psyche; so fervent, your mind surrenders to them almost naturally; so consuming, that there's nothing else you could even think to think about…

Burn

We were once the soft
light playing on prisms
creating rainbows.
A euphony for the eyes
Now I am the scorching sun
one march noon
Burning with the tenacity
To bring the mighty oak forest on its knees;
Ashes beneath my feet

– the contempt in me

Caution

I pick up the remnants of me scattered smithereens
Strewn
across the past…
and now
Collapsed
by the multiple blows
of you.
You?
Corked like a cosmic supernova
in a glass bottle,
wired to erupt.
And me?
Hoping you came
with a caution sign…

– collateral damage of hoping against the hopen hope

With You, Once Again

I met us again in the dim-lit alleyways
Of age-old albums with pictures, we clicked
With your brother's paper camera
Under the Christmas mistletoe

I met us again in the pages of that book
From the store where we first met
In the corners of the pressed daisies
That I treasured in those stories

I met us daily in the nooks and niches of my life
Again and again, facing you
My mind tries to lose you each day
But I find you again in the vestiges
My heart clutches to, each night.

And We Still Live On

Dear Donna,
I brought peonies,
just like you asked.
Shaved but not too much,
just like you asked;
Put on that blush-hued shirt,
just like you asked…

Brought that video of us
On our wedding day
Saying "till death do us part"
I could run and stop them
But time tackles me down
Leaving me trapped behind
The bars of our present.

I wait for you…
Lay down the mat
It's the crack of dawn
And I know you won't come.
So, I lie down and watch alone
In front of the stone, I carved myself
"Here lies Donna Grey"

I know you can't come,
But you could send me some sun
These wilted flowers may live on
And so will you
for I'll know you come here too
our very own vows
Like after we said,
"I do"

Tryst of the Times

HIM

As majestic as a prince in an ancient jest,
With eyes the blue of ocean waves,
Effused with cheer, oozing with zest,
Glowing with such vigour that the heavens shy away

HER

A dark mystery, enigmatic and abstruse,
Delphic like time with secrets like the moon
Intimidating like death, mystifying like a rune
A conundrum nobody could deduce

THEM

They watched each other passively,
With building intent and an incessant pull
A glaring truth agonized their souls relentlessly
They knew it all too well and the world too
The dusk and dawn were never meant to be.

6

La Rose – The Shade of New Wonder

Birth… the beginning; the very first moment, the first spark, the first caress, the first smile.

Pink is the shade of new life – the flower bud barely unfurled, the tinted skin of a newborn baby, the sky before the sun rises, and before the stars too... The colour of the beautiful, the novel, the wondrous, the magical. For me, it also stands for the new love, just born. The kind that is still mid-bloom, pure, true. The good parts of it, the butterflies, the dates, the conversations that keep your heart awake later than the stars, the charm which enchants your mind. Pink or *la rose* – the shade of all things beautiful… of the beautiful moments, the ones we wish should last forever; of beautiful memories, the ones you hope you can always keep close; and of beautiful people, the ones you know truly care for you.

Miles Apart

That day, that room, those moments, and those stolen smiles
A shower of sun rays lit up those pools of liquid light
And how they delved in my heart and made my soul beam…
Like mere wisps of smoke, the others just seemed to fade away

Said some words my heart still clutches too tight
Scribbled those digits now engraved in my mind
We did walk away and we did say goodbye
With our very blue hearts under the very grey sky

I remember the first hello and my gleaming eyes, my fluttering heart
And my face the red of the sundown sky
I remember those late nights, we spent just a screen apart
The thought of that mischievous smile playing on your lips
Driving my sleep away!
And I remember each word you said, that brought us closer
Our hearts nestled together yet ourselves so far away.

Miles apart, your words embraced me like no hug ever could
Miles apart, your smile still made me smile, no matter how far you stood
Miles apart, you still lit up my day, even though we lived them far away.
Miles apart, an 'us' did exist; even if far we lay.

Unaware

The stars that gaze us each night
Know how oblivious we are of our very own hearts;
The moon that shines on us, soft and silver
Knows how we attain solace only in each other's words;
The winds of time that pass us by
Know we discover each other more bit by bit,
with every second that flutters by.
Each time we are at peace
each time we are content
each time we are hand in hand
the universe holds its breath
waiting for us to realize –
our very own infinity.

Falling In Love

To fall in love with you
Was like a peach-tinted sunset.
On one September evening
When the sky was a stained-glass melody
Holding its breath for admiration

It began with a few threads of pink
astray in my heart creeping in
when those pools of warm light
caught my eyes
The very first time.

The hues of ecstasy and wonder and magic
Spread to every inch of the canvas
of my little universe
until it became a part of me.
It started slowly, quietly, gradually
but then swiftly
flew me to a night
of the stars and moon and
and you.

A Feeling Called Home

I caged myself in four walls of mortar and doubt and fear
Of stepping out of this conclave of all of my insecurities.
I was strewn across the cold hard marble ground; tangled.
But you held me close and made me shine like
A decked-up tree with Christmas lights.

I froze in the ice-laden snowscapes built over years
from bitter rulings of the court of life,
Piercing icicles ruptured my theory of me
but you scooped me in and put me back
Like a young boy doing a jigsaw
Piece by piece.

I was listless and astray in the braided alleyways
Of time and death and grief
Like a vagabond in a desert,
With blistered feet and a parched throat
But falling in love with you
Was like coming back home
To entrancing breaths of
Vanilla and cinnamon
And you.

7 La Jaune – The Shade of a Promise

A promise is a mysterious entity in the spheres of the heart, built on faith and trust. The bravest of emotions, the ones which require sheer courage. For us to strip out of every other betrayal we have been inflicted with, and extend our arms like a baby in his brand-new world. To let the brick-walled citadel we've caged ourselves in fade into oblivion and step out with hope, and a promise. It is the toughest thing people in love do. Bards have said time and again, that "love is dangerous" or "love is scary" but in absolute honesty, I do not believe that it's loving that scares lovers. It's the act of trust, the hope of culmination of a promise and the fear that it won't. But love is not the only place where promises thrive, we make promises to ourselves too – to do better, to fight our demons, to wake up each day and be our best selves. Yellow or *la jaune* is the shade of fulfilled promises or the hope that they will be fulfilled; of trust in others and ourselves; of self-discovery, liberation, freedom, exploration, of a hope that time will keep its promise of being better… of a new tomorrow that shines on the horizon.

Her

Looking in the mirror, I see her
Whose eyes hide tears only her ink can construe
Whose lips veil secrets only her words can say
And whose heart lacks light only her pieces can reflect

Each time she lifts her quill, each time she pens her heart
She spills herself in those pages
only to discover her psyche
She confines her demons in that diary
only to not have to see them again
She lives like that doused sun,
only to burn brighter and brighter after.

She fills not just pages, she reflects her mind
She pens not just verses, she portrays her Self
She lives her each piece, she wakes up wiser
For she writes not just words but inks her being

One and Free

With a storm in my head and wind in my hair
through the drift days and the sway of seconds
I search for a key to soaring skies
only to lose it in the clouds there

Locked in a cage reminiscing what I was once
all around me, glaring sun blinds what I could see
yet I sit here in this town when no light reaches me
these chains around my soul force myself out of me
each link made up of my sins and my impiety

I am a mosaic of unsolved puzzles
Waiting for the caress of thought and scrutiny
And so, I build a way out of this labyrinth
To the beyond and farther, where my Self knows me.
Where my mind runs free in the fields of hope
Where my heart swims in joy in the
boundless bounty of dreams;
Where my face is just one and not masked
under years of manipulated nudges,
Where I am one, and free…

A New World

the clock strikes 12
a robin snips the
yarn of my slumber
and the sky is painted in ivory
and gold and hope
like a fresh canvas
out of a tiny workshop
on the cobblestone street
the air is heavy
with butter and sugar
and dreams
as the baker bakes marvels
for this new world
I step out to see
Time preening
its feathers of novelty
under the gold rays of a promise
but these rays will part
and the sun will rest its carriage
in the barracks of the horses
which pull the moon
but worry not o child

for the clock will strike 12 once more
the sky will strip bare of its hues once more
the blades of grass will shed their moist pearls once more…
The time may have surrendered to senility last night
but it will rise like a raging phoenix
once more
once more